A SIMPLE SERIES EASTER

PRESENTS

THE BLOOD WILL NEVER LOSE ITS POWER

A 27-MINUTE MINI MUSICAL

Arranged Especially for Unison/2-Part Choir

CREATED BY

Johnathan Crumpton and Luke Gambill

AVAILABLE PRODUCTS:

Choral Book	45757-2312-7
CD Preview Pak	45757-2312-1
Listening CD	45757-2312-2
Split-Track Accompaniment CD	45757-2312-3
Split-Track Accompaniment DVD	45757-2312-6
Soprano/Alto Rehearsal Track CD	45757-2312-0
Tenor/Bass Rehearsal Track CD	45757-2312-5

 BRENTWOOD MUSIC PUBLICATIONS a division of BRENTWOOD-BENSON music publications www.brentwoodbenson.com

CONTENTS

Jesus Is Alive Medley
Jesus Is Alive *with* Christ Arose

Arranged by Russell Mauldin

JESUS IS ALIVE (Ron Kenoly)

Hal - le - lu - jah!___ Je - sus is a - live!___ Death has lost its vic-

5

6

37

lu - jah! Je - sus is a - live!

E♭maj7   Cm7   E♭/F   F   E♭/F   F   B♭   E♭2/F

41   CHRIST AROSE (Robert Lowry)

Up from the grave He a - rose   with a

B♭   Dm/A   Gm   Gm9/F   Gm/F

45

might - y   tri - umph o'er His   foes.   He a -

E♭maj7   F/E♭   Dm7   Gm7   Gm/F

49

rose   a   vic - tor from the dark do - main,   and He

C/E   E♭m6   B♭2/D   Cm7   B♭

Je - sus is a - live!

Death has lost its vic - t'ry, and the grave has been de - nied.

Je - sus lives for - ev - er, He's a -

live! He's a - live!

Rugged Cross Medley
The Old Rugged Cross *with* My Jesus, I Love Thee

Arranged by Russell Mauldin

NARRATOR: Hallelujah, Jesus is alive! Through the cross of Christ, everything that kept us bound has been destroyed. *(Music starts)* Everything that would have separated us from God has been defeated. And every promise of abundant life has become ours.

THE OLD RUGGED CROSS (George Bennard)

On a hill far a-way stood an old rug-ged cross, the em-blem of suf-'ring and shame.

12

till my tro - phies at last I lay down.

I will cling to the old rug - ged

cross_____ and ex - change it some -

day for a crown.

14

MY JESUS, I LOVE THEE (William R. Featherston, Adoniram J. Gordon)

cross_____ and ex - change it some - day_____ for a crown._____

MEN sing cue notes **mp**

My Je - sus, I love_____ Thee, I

We Remember

Words and Music by
SUE C. SMITH and RONNIE FREEMAN
Arranged by Cliff Duren

NARRATOR: On Thursday before His crucifixion, Jesus sent Peter and John to prepare the Passover meal. That evening, *(Music starts)* the Master looked around at His friends, men who still had so much to understand. He looked into the eyes of the one who would betray Him and one who would deny Him, knowing all of them would desert Him in a few hours. Even though His heart was heavy because of what lay ahead, Jesus lovingly gave them a way to remember Him always.

live be - cause You died._____

We re - mem - ber_____ we be - long to

You_____ and You make all things new.

We re - mem - ber._____ We live un - a -

Nothing but the Blood Underscore
(Responsive Reading)

Arranged by Cliff Duren

NARRATOR: Please stand and read responsively with me from Hebrews. *(Music starts)*

Christ has now become the High Priest over all the good things that have come. With His own blood – not the blood of goats and calves – He entered the Most Holy Place once for all time and secured our redemption forever.

CONGREGATION: Christ offered Himself to God as a perfect sacrifice for our sins.

NARRATOR: That is why He is the One who mediates a new covenant between God and people, so that all who are called can receive the eternal inheritance God has promised them.

CONGREGATION: For Christ died to set them free from the penalty of the sins they had committed under that first covenant.

NARRATOR: That is why even the first covenant was put into effect with the blood of an animal. In fact, according to the law of Moses, nearly everything was purified with blood.

CONGREGATION: For without the shedding of blood, there is no forgiveness.

NARRATOR: And just as each person is destined to die once and after that comes judgment, so also Christ died once for all time as a sacrifice to take away the sins of many people.

CONGREGATION: He will come again, not to deal with our sins, but to bring salvation to all who are eagerly waiting for Him.

NARRATOR: Please be seated.

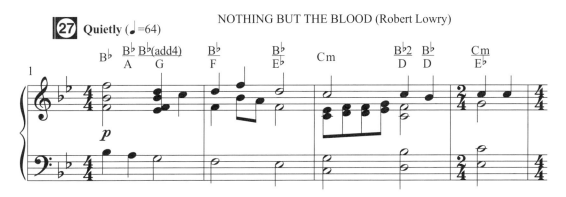

NOTHING BUT THE BLOOD (Robert Lowry)

28

JESUS PAID IT ALL (John T. Grape)

O the Blood
with Nothing but the Blood

Words and Music by
MARY ELIZABETH MILLER
and THOMAS MILLER
Arranged by Cliff Duren

30

SOLOIST may continue with Choir to the end

NOTHING BUT THE BLOOD (Robert Lowry)

The Blood Will Never Lose Its Power

Words and Music by
ANDRAÉ CROUCH
Arranged by Russell Mauldin

NARRATOR: Christ had come to be more than a King. He was born into our world to become our Savior.

(Music starts) In His blood, was power: power to forgive, to cleanse and heal, to overcome, and to live a life of victory!

lose its pow'r. It will nev - er, nev - er, it will nev - er lose its pow'r, nev-er lose its pow'r!

Jesus Is Alive (Finale)

Words and Music by
RON KENOLY
Arranged by Russell Mauldin

NARRATOR: At noon on the day of His crucifixion, the darkness was so great that it was like midnight. How hopeless and final it all seemed. However …

(Music starts) Early on Sunday morning, some women who had followed Jesus during His ministry went to the tomb before dawn to anoint His body. But their spices went unused and forgotten because instead of finding His broken body, they discovered an empty tomb and an angel who told them, "Jesus isn't here. He's alive! Go and tell Peter and the rest of His disciples."

Death had been conquered by the cross! His precious blood will never lose its power, and the grave has been swallowed up by His victory! Hallelujah! Jesus is alive!

48